Bernard Pomerance

THE ELEPHANT MAN
A Drama

Introduction and Notes by Ray Speakman

HEINEMANN
EDUCATIONAL

Heinemann Educational
a division of
Heinemann Educational Books Ltd
Halley Court, Jordan Hill, Oxford OX2 8EJ
OXFORD LONDON EDINBURGH
MADRID ATHENS BOLOGNA PARIS
MELBOURNE SYDNEY AUCKLAND
IBADAN NAIROBI HARARE GABORONE
SINGAPORE TOKYO PORTSMOUTH NH (USA)

First published in 1979 by Samuel French Inc.
First published in this edition by Heinemann Educational 1991

92 93 94 95 96 11 10 9 8 7 6 5 4 3 2

ISBN 0 435 22587 1

Printed in England by Clays Ltd, St Ives plc

Contents

Introduction   v

THE ELEPHANT MAN   1

Activities and Explorations   55
   Keeping Track   55
   Explorations   60
   Essays   64

INTRODUCTION

The play

Bernard Pomerance's play, *The Elephant Man*, was first performed in 1977 by the Foco Novo Theatre Company at the Hampstead Theatre. In 1981 a film of the same name was made by the American director, David Lynch. In fact, the film, although also based upon the true story of John Merrick, has no connection with the play as it points out at the end of the final credits.

John Merrick was born hideously deformed in the late nineteenth century. He was exhibited as a freak in a travelling show until discovered by a doctor, Frederick Treves, who removed him to the London Hospital for scientific study. Treves's story was first told in 1923 in his book, *The Elephant Man and Other Reminiscences* (Cassell). His account was given again in *The Elephant Man, A Study in Human Dignity* by Ashley Montague (Ballantine Books, 1973). This later work contains photographs of John Merrick and of the model he made of St Phillip's Church. It is the accounts given in these two works which form the basis of film and play. Having said that, there are clear differences in the two works.

David Lynch's film seems to have taken as its starting point the idea of 'a study in human dignity' which was the theme of Ashley Montague's book. John Hurt, who played the 'Elephant Man', presented a realistic depiction of Merrick's appearance and speech. The script, by Eric Bergren, Christopher De Vore and Lynch himself, concentrated upon Merrick's struggle to survive in the face of public hostility, largely represented by a sadistic hospital porter played by Michael Elphick. Despite his awful disabilities and the insensitivity of many of those he meets, Merrick battles to maintain his dignity and his desire to live like, and be treated like a human being. As Frederick Treves, Anthony Hopkins learns about human dignity as he teaches Merrick about London society. His chief dilemma arises from the suspicion that he is using Merrick to further his own career in much the same way as the sideshow owner had exhibited Merrick for his own profit.

The play is more complex. There is no attempt to represent Merrick's appearance realistically or to reproduce his speech difficulties on the stage. The audience are shown the real Merrick on a screen (in photographs), and the actor confines his presentation of the 'Elephant Man' to an indication of his movement. Bernard Pomerance believed that any attempt to 'reproduce his speech and appearance . . . would seem to me not only counter-productive, but, the more remarkably successful, the more distracting from the play'. There would also be, of course, the practical difficulty in the theatre of a central actor with a speech difficulty.

More important than these practicalities are the central themes of the play. Clearly it is not concerned with the shock value of Merrick's disabilities, as it might be argued the film is, but with more complex issues. The portrayal of Treves is much more central to the play than it is to the film. His initial concern, once he has 'rescued' Merrick, and once his scientific curiosity is satisfied, is to transform Merrick into a good Victorian. Although surprised and delighted by Merrick's sensitivity and intelligence, he goes on to patronise him, to teach him the social graces as one would a child. He fails to see that Merrick is a man and as such is an equal. This is highlighted in the play through the character of Mrs Kendall who recognises Merrick as a man like any other man, and also perceives Treves's constricted emotions. It becomes increasingly clear as the play progresses that Treves cannot cope with his own humanity, let alone other people's.

Through his success with John Merrick, Treves becomes well known and the London Hospital is a fashionable centre for London society. Despite his success and his nagging doubts about his 'use' of John, Treves's central worries turn more and more towards the nature of Victorian society. This is wonderfully shown in scenes seventeen and eighteen where, in a dream, Treves and Merrick reverse roles – and it is Treves and his society who are shown as disabled, trapped, self-destructive and emotionally ugly. The morality by which they live is a sham.

The play in the classroom

The text of the play is a rich source for classroom discussion and writing. The suggestions in **Keeping Track** and the essay titles which are presented after the text in this edition provide a support for study. A comparison of the play and the film (available widely in video shops) would further enrich a study of the text.

It would be a pity, however, to stop there. The play opens up wider issues to do with society's attitudes to the disabled – and to other disadvantaged groups in our own contemporary society. It is a challenging piece and, like all such writing, when used in the classroom it requires the teacher to take a positive rather than a passive role. We all need to face the questions asked by Bernard Pomerance through his creation of Frederick Treves. Some ideas are presented for the teacher's consideration in the section **Explorations** given after the text, but as with all such extension work the teacher knows best how to handle delicate or disturbing questions with particular groups of students. As is often the case with work of this sort, it is often helpful to seek the advice and support of the local Social Services.

Ray Speakman

Acknowledgement

The ideas for the short plays contained in **Exploration (6)** are freely adapted from Anne Wilkinson's book, *It's Not Fair*: *a handbook on World Development* published by Christian Aid (1985).

THE ELEPHANT MAN

CHARACTERS

FREDERICK TREVES, *a surgeon and teacher*
CARR GOMM, *administrator of the London Hospital*
ROSS, *Manager of the Elephant Man*
JOHN MERRICK, *the Elephant Man*
Three PINHEADS, *three women freaks whose heads are pointed*
BELGIAN POLICEMEN
LONDON POLICEMAN
MAN, *at a fairground in Brussels*
CONDUCTOR, *of Ostend-London boat train*
BISHOP WALSHAM HOW
PORTER, *at the London Hospital*
SNORK, *also a porter*
MRS KENDAL, *an actress*
DUCHESS
COUNTESS
PRINCESS ALEXANDRA
LORD JOHN
NURSE, MISS SANDWICH

1884–1890. London. One scene is in Belgium.

HE WILL HAVE 100 GUINEA
FEES BEFORE HE'S FORTY

The London Hospital, Whitechapel Rd. Enter GOMM, *enter*
TREVES.

TREVES: Mr Carr Gomm? Frederick Treves. Your new
lecturer in anatomy.

GOMM: Age thirty-one. Books on Scrofula and Applied
Surgical Anatomy – I'm happy to see you rising, Mr
Treves. I like to see merit credited, and your industry,
accomplishment, and skill all do you credit. Ignore the
squalor of Whitechapel, the general dinginess, neglect
and poverty without, and you will find a continual
medical richesse in the London Hospital. We study and
treat the widest range of diseases and disorders, and are
certainly the greatest institution of our kind in the world.
The Empire provides unparalleled opportunities for our
studies, as places cruel to life are the most revealing
scientifically. Add to our reputation by going further,
and that'll satisfy. You've bought a house?

TREVES: On Wimpole Street.

GOMM: Good. Keep at it, Treves. You'll have an FRS and
100 guinea fees before you're forty. You'll find it is an
excellent consolation prize.

TREVES: Consolation? I don't know what you mean.

GOMM: I know you don't. You will (*Exits*).

TREVES: A happy childhood in Dorset.

A scientist in an age of science.

In an English age, an Englishman. A teacher and a

3

doctor at the London. Two books published by my thirty-first year. A house. A wife who loves me, and my god, 100 guinea fees before I'm forty.

Consolation for what?

As of the year AD 1884, I, Freddie Treves, have excessive blessings. Or so it seems to me.

Blackout.

SCENE 2

ART IS AS NOTHING TO NATURE

Whitechapel Rd. A storefront. A large advertisement of a creature with an elephant's head. ROSS, *his manager.*

ROSS: Tuppence only, step in and see: This side of the grave, John Merrick has no hope nor expectation of relief. In every sense his situation is desperate. His physical agony is exceeded only by his mental anguish, a despised creature without consolation. Tuppence only, step in and see! To live with his physical hideousness, incapacitating deformities and unremitting pain is trial enough, but to be exposed to the cruelly lacerating expressions of horror and disgust by all who behold him – is even more difficult to bear. Tuppence only, step in and see! For in order to survive, Merrick forces himself to suffer these humiliations, I repeat, humiliations, in order to survive, thus he exposes himself to crowds who pay to gape and yawp at this freak of nature, the Elephant Man.

Enter TREVES *who looks at advertisement.*

ROSS: See Mother Nature uncorseted and in malignant rage! Tuppence.

TREVES: This sign's absurd. Half-elephant, half-man is not possible. Is he foreign?

ROSS. Right, from Leicester. But nothing to fear.

TREVES: I'm at the London across the road. I would be curious to see him if there is some genuine disorder. If he is a mass of papier-mâché and paint however –

ROSS: Then pay me nothing. Enter, sir. Merrick, stand up. Ya bloody donkey, up, up.

They go in, then emerge. TREVES *pays.*

TREVES: I must examine him further at the hospital. Here is my card. I'm Treves. I will have a cab pick him up and return him. My card will gain him admittance.

ROSS: Five bob he's yours for the day.

TREVES: I wish to examine him in the interests of science, you see.

ROSS: Sir, I'm Ross. I look out for him, get him his living. Found him in Leicester workhouse. His own ma put him there age of three. Couldn't bear the sight, well you can see why. We – he and I – are in business. He is our capital, see. Go to a bank. Go anywhere. Want to borrow capital, you pay interest. Scientists even. He's good value though. You won't find another like him.

TREVES. Fair enough. (*He pays*).

ROSS: Right. out here, Merrick. Ya bloody donkey, out!

Lights fade out.

Scene 3

WHO HAS SEEN THE LIKE OF THIS?

TREVES *lectures.* MERRICK *contorts himself to approximate projected slides of the real Merrick.*

TREVES. The most striking feature about him was his enormous head. Its circumference was about that of a man's waist. From the brow there projected a huge bony mass like a loaf, while from the back of his head hung a bag of spongy fungous-looking skin, the surface of which was comparable to brown cauliflower. On the top of the skull were a few long lank hairs. The osseous growth on the forehead, at this stage about the size of a tangerine, almost occluded one eye. From the upper jaw there projected another mass of bone. It protruded from the mouth like a pink stump, turning the upper lip inside out, and making the mouth a wide slobbering aperture. The nose was merely a lump of flesh, only recognizable as a nose from its position. The deformities rendered the face utterly incapable of the expression of any emotion whatsoever. The back was horrible because from it hung, as far down as the middle of the thigh, huge sacklike masses of flesh covered by the same loathsome cauliflower stain. The right arm was of enourmous size and shapless. It suggested but was not elephantiasis, and was overgrown also with pendant masses of the same cauliflower-like skin. The right hand was large and clumsy – a fin or paddle rather than a hand. No distinction existed between the palm and back, the thumb was like a radish, the fingers like thick tuberous roots. As a limb it was useless. The other arm was remarkable by contrast. It was not only normal, but was moreover a delicately shaped limb covered with a fine skin and provided with a beautiful hand which any woman might have envied. From the chest hung a bag of the same repulsive flesh. It was like a dewlap suspended from the neck of a lizard. The lower limbs had the characters of the deformed arm. They were unwieldy, dropsical-looking, and grossly mis-shapen. There arose from the fungous skin growths a very sickening stench which was hard to tolerate. To add a further burden to his trouble, the wretched man when a boy developed a hip disease which left him permanently lame, so that he could only walk with a stick. (*To* MERRICK.) Please. (MERRICK *walks*.) He was thus denied all means of escape from his tormentors.

VOICE: Mr Treves, you have shown a profound and unknown disorder to us. You have said when he leaves here it is for his exhibition again. I do not think it ought to be permitted. It is a disgrace. It is a pity and a disgrace. It is an indecency in fact. It may be a danger in ways we do not know. Something ought to be done about it.

TREVES: I am a doctor. What would you have me do?

VOICE: Well. I know what to do. *I* know.

Silence. A policeman enters as lights fade out.

SCENE 4

THIS INDECENCY MAY NOT CONTINUE

Music. A fair. PINHEADS *huddling together, holding a portrait of Leopold, King of the Congo. Enter* MAN.

MAN: Now my pinheaded darlings, your attention please. Every freak in Brussels Fair is doing something to celebrate Leopold's fifth year as King of the Congo. Him. Our King. Our Empire. (*They begin reciting.*) No, don't recite yet, you morons. I'll say when. And when you do, get it *right*. You don't, it's back to the asylum. Know what that means, don't you? They'll cut your heads. They'll spoon out your little brains, replace 'em in the dachshund they were nicked from. *Cut you.* Yeah. Be back with customers. Come see the Queens of the Congo! (*Exits.*)

Enter MERRICK, ROSS.

MERRICK: Cosmos? Cosmos?
ROSS: Congo. Land of darkness. Hoho! (*Sees* PINS.) Look at them, lad. It's freer on the continent. Loads of indecency here, no one minds. You won't get coppers sent round to roust you out like London. Reckon in Brussels here's our fortune. You have a little tête-à-tête with this lot while I see the coppers about our licence to exhibit. Be right back. (*Exits.*)
MERRICK: I come from England.
ROSS: Allo!
MERRICK: At home they chased us. Out of London. Police. Someone complained. They beat me. You have no trouble? No?

PINS: Allo! Allo!

MERRICK: Hello. In Belgium we make money. I look forward to it. Happiness, I mean. You pay your police? How is it done?

PINS: Allo! Allo!

MERRICK: We do a show together sometime? Yes? I have saved forty-eight pounds. Two shillings. Nine pence. English money. Ross takes care of it.

PINS: Allo! Allo!

MERRICK: Little vocabulary problem, eh? Poor things. Looks like they put your noses to the grindstone and forgot to take them away.

MAN *enters.*

MAN: They're coming. (*People enter to see the girls' act.*) Now.

PINS: (*Dancing and singing*):

> We are the Queens of the Congo,
> The Beautiful Belgian empire
> Our niggers are bigger
> Our miners are finer
> Empire, Empire, Congo and power
> Civilizuzu's finest hour
> Admire, perspire, desire, acquire
> Or we'll set you on fire!

MAN: You cretins! Sorry, they're not ready yet. Out please. (*People exit.*) Get those words right, girls! Or you know what. (MAN *exits.* PINS *weep.*)

MERRICK: Don't cry. You sang nicely. Don't cry. There there.

Enter ROSS *in grip of two* POLICEMEN.

ROSS: I was promised a permit. I lined a tour up on that!

POLICEMEN: This is a brutal, indecent, and immoral display. It is a public indecency, and it is forbidden here.

ROSS: What about them with their perfect cone heads?

POLICEMEN: They are ours.

ROSS: Competition's good for business. Where's your spirit of competition?

POLICEMEN: Right here. (*Smacks* MERRICK).

ROSS: DON'T DO THAT, YOU'LL KILL HIM!

POLICEMEN: Be better off dead. Indecent bastard.

MERRICK: Don't cry girls. Doesn't hurt.

PINS: Indecent, indecent, indecent, indecent!!

> POLICEMEN *escort* MERRICK *and* ROSS *out, i.e., forward.*
> *Blackout except spot on* MERRICK *and* ROSS.

MERRICK: Ostend will always mean bad memories. Won't it, Ross?

ROSS: I've decided. I'm sending you back, lad. You're a flop. No, you're a liability. You ain't the moneymaker I figured, so that's it.

MERRICK: Alone?

ROSS: Here's a few bob, have a nosh. I'm keeping the rest. For my trouble. I deserve it, I reckon. Invested enough with you. Pick up your stink if I stick around. Stink of failure. Stink of lost years. Just stink, stink, stink, stink, stink.

> *Enter* CONDUCTOR.

CONDUCTOR: This the one?

ROSS: Just see him to Liverpool St Station safe, will you? Here's for your trouble.

MERRICK: Robbed.

CONDUCTOR: What's he say?

ROSS: Just makes sounds. Fella's an imbecile.

MERRICK: Robbed.

ROSS: Bon voyage, Johnny. His name is Johnny. He knows his name, that's all, though.

CONDUCTOR: Don't follow him, Johnny. Johnny, come on boat now. Conductor find Johnny place out of sight. Johnny! Johnny! Don't struggle, Johnny. Johnny come on.

MERRICK: Robbed! Robbed!

Fadeout on struggle.

SCENE 5

POLICE SIDE WITH IMBECILE AGAINST THE CROWD

Darkness. Uproar, shouts.

VOICE: Liverpool St Station!

Enter MERRICK, CONDUCTOR, POLICEMAN.

POLICEMAN: We're safe in here. I barred the door.

CONDUCTOR: They wanted to rip him to pieces. I've never seen anything like it. It was like being Gordon at bleedin' Khartoum.

POLICEMAN: Got somewhere to go in London, lad? Can't stay here.

11

CONDUCTOR: He's an imbecile. He don't understand. Search him.

POLICEMAN: Got any money?

MERRICK: Robbed.

POLICEMAN: What's that?

CONDUCTOR: He just makes sounds. Frightened sounds is all he makes. Go through his coat.

MERRICK: Je-sus.

POLICEMAN: Don't let me go through your coat, I'll turn you over to that lot! Oh, I was joking, don't upset yourself.

MERRICK: Joke? Joke?

POLICEMAN: Sure, croak, croak, croak, croak.

MERRICK: Je-sus.

POLICEMAN: Got a card here. You Johnny Merrick? What's this old card here, Johnny? Someone give you a card?

CONDUCTOR: What's it say?

POLICEMAN: Says Mr Frederick Treves, Lecturer in Anatomy, the London Hospital.

CONDUCTOR: I'll go see if I can find him, its not far. (*Exits.*)

POLICEMAN: What's he do, lecture you on your anatomy? People who think right don't look like that then, do they? Yeah, glung, glung, glung, glung.

MERRICK: Jesus. Jesus.

POLICEMAN: Sure, Treves, Treves, Treves, Treves.

Blackout, then lights go up as CONDUCTOR *leads* TREVES *in.*

TREVES: What is going on here? Look at that mob, have you no sense of decency? I am Frederick Treves. This is my card.

POLICEMAN: This poor wretch here had it. Arrived from Ostend.

TREVES: Good Lord, Merrick? John Merrick? What has happened to you?

MERRICK: Help me!

Fadeout.

SCENE 6

EVEN ON THE NIGER AND CEYLON, NOT THIS

The London Hospital. MERRICK *in bathtub.* TREVES *outside. Enter* MISS SANDWICH.

TREVES: You are? Miss Sandwich?

SANDWICH: Sandwich. Yes.

TREVES: You have had experience in missionary hospitals in the Niger.

SANDWICH: And Ceylon.

TREVES: I may assume you've seen –

SANDWICH: The tropics. Oh those diseases. The many and the awful scourges our Lord sends, yes, sir.

TREVES: I need the help of an experienced nurse, you see.

SANDWICH: Someone to bring him food, take care of the room. Yes, I understand. But it is somehow difficult.

TREVES: Well, I have been let down so far. He really is – that is, the regular sisters – well, it is not part of their job and they will not do it. Be ordinarily kind to Mr Merrick.

13

Without – well – panicking. He is quite beyond ugly. You understand that? His appearance has terrified them.

SANDWICH: The photographs show a terrible disease.

TREVES: It is a disorder, not a disease; it is in no way contagious though we don't in fact know what it is. I have found however that there is a deep superstition in those I've tried, they actually believe he somehow brought it on himself, this thing, and of course it is not that at all.

SANDWICH: I am not one who believes it is ourselves who attain grace or bring chastisement to us, sir.

TREVES: Miss Sandwich, I am hoping not.

SANDWICH: Let me put your mind to rest. Care for lepers in the East, and you have cared, Mr Treves. In Africa, I have seen dreadful scourges quite unknown to our more civilized climes. What at home could be worse than a miserable and afflicted rotting black?

TREVES: I imagine.

SANDWICH: Appearances do not daunt me.

TREVES: It is really that that has sent me outside the confines of the London seeking help.

SANDWICH: 'I look unto the hills whence cometh my help.' I understand: I think I will be satisfactory.

Enter PORTER *with tray.*

PORTER: His lunch. (*Exits*).

TREVES: Perhaps you would be so kind as to accompany me this time. I will introduce you.

SANDWICH: Allow me to carry the tray.

TREVES: I will this time. You are ready.

SANDWICH: I am.

TREVES: He is bathing to be rid of his odour. (*They enter to* MERRICK.) John, this is Miss Sandwich. She –

SANDWICH: I – (*Unable to control herself.*) Oh my good God in heaven. (*Bolts room.*)

TREVES: (*Puts* MERRICK'S *lunch down.*) I am sorry. I thought –

MERRICK: Thank you for saving the lunch this time.

TREVES: Excuse me. (*Exits to Miss sandwich.*) You have let me down, you know. I did everything to warn you and still you let me down.

SANDWICH: You didn't say.

TREVES: But I –

SANDWICH: Didn't! You said – just words!

TREVES: But the photographs.

SANDWICH: Just pictures. No one will do this. I am sorry. (*Exits*).

TREVES: Yes. Well. this is not helping him.

Fadeout.

SCENE 7

THE ENGLISH PUBLIC WILL PAY FOR HIM TO BE LIKE US

The London Hospital. MERRICK *in a bathtub reading.* TREVES, BISHOP HOW *in foreground.*

BISHOP: With what fortitude he bears his cross! It is remarkable. He has made the acquaintance of religion

15

and knows sections of the Bible by heart. Once I'd grasped his speech, it became clear he'd certainly had religious instruction at one time.

TREVES: I believe it was in the workhouse, Dr How.

BISHOP: They are awfully good about that sometimes. The psalms he loves, and the book of Job perplexes him, he says, for he cannot see that a just God must cause suffering, as he puts it, merely then to be merciful. Yet that Christ will save him he does not doubt, so he is not resentful.

Enters GOMM.

GOMM: Christ had better; be dammed if we can.

BISHOP: Ahem. In any case Dr Treves, he has a religious nature, further instruction would uplift him and I'd be pleased to provide it. I plan to speak of him from the pulpit this week.

GOMM: I see our visiting bather has flushed the busy Bishop How from his cruciform lair.

BISHOP: Speak with Merrick, sir. I have spoken to him of Mercy and Justice. There's a true Christian in the rough.

GOMM: This makes my news seem banal, yet: Frederick, the response to my letter to the *Times* about Merrick has been staggering. The English public has been so generous that Merrick may be supported for life without a penny spent from Hospital funds.

TREVES: But that is excellent.

BISHOP: God bless the English public.

GOMM: Especially for not dismembering him at Liverpool St Station. Freddie, the London's no home for incurables, this is quite irregular, but for you I permit it – though god knows what you'll do.

BISHOP: God does know, sir, and Darwin does not.

GOMM: He'd better, sir; he deformed him.

BISHOP: I had apprehensions coming here. I find it most fortunate Merrick is in the hands of Dr Treves, a Christian, sir.

GOMM: Freddie is a good man and a brilliant doctor, and that is fortunate indeed.

TREVES: I couldn't have raised the funds though, Doctor.

BISHOP: Don't let me keep you longer from your duties, Mr Treves. Yet, Mr Gomm, consider: is it science, sir, that motivates us when we transport English rule of law to India or Ireland? When good British churchmen leave hearth and home for missionary hardship in Africa, is it science that bears them away? Sir it is not. It is Christian duty. It is the obligation to bring our light and benefices to benighted man. That motivates us, even as it motivates Treves toward Merrick, sir, to bring salvation where none is. Gordon was a Christian, sir, and died at Khartoum for it. Not for science, sir.

GOMM: You're telling me, not for science.

BISHOP: Mr Treves, I'll visit Merrick weekly if I may.

TREVES: You will be welcome, sir, I am certain.

BISHOP: Then good day, sirs. (*Exits*).

GOMM: Well, Jesus my boy, now we have the money, what do you plan for Merrick?

TREVES: Normality as far as possible.

GOMM: So he will be like us? Ah. (*Smiles*.)

TREVES: Is something wrong, Mr Gomm? With us?

Fadeout.

Scene 8

MERCY AND JUSTICE ELUDE
OUR MINDS AND ACTIONS

MERRICK *in bath.* TREVES, GOMM.

MERRICK: How long is as long as I like?

TREVES: You may stay for life. The funds exist.

MERRICK: Been reading this. About homes for the blind.
  Wouldn't mind going to one when I have to move.

TREVES: But you do not have to move; and you're not blind.

MERRICK: I would prefer it where no one stared at me.

GOMM: No one will bother you here.

TREVES: Certainly not. I've given instructions.

  PORTER *and* SNORK *peek in.*

PORTER: What'd I tell you?

SNORK: Gawd almighty. Oh. Mr Treves. Mr Gomm.

TREVES: You were told not to do this. I don't understand.
  You must not lurk about. Surely you have work?

PORTER: Yes, sir.

TREVES: Well, it is infuriating. When you are told a thing,
  you must listen. I won't have you gaping in on my
  patients. Kindly remember that.

PORTER: Isn't a patient, sir, is he?

TREVES: Do not let me find you here again.

PORTER: Didn't know you were here, sir. We'll be off now.

GOMM: No, no, Will. Mr Treves was precisely saying no
  one would intrude when you intruded.

TREVES: He is warned now. Merrick does not like it.

GOMM: He was warned before. On what penalty, Will?

PORTER: That you'd sack me, sir.

GOMM: You are sacked, Will. You, his friend, you work here?

SNORK: Just started last week, sir.

GOMM: Well, I hope the point is taken now.

PORTER: Mr Gomm – I ain't truly sacked, am I?

GOMM: Will, yes. Truly sacked. You will never be more truly sacked.

PORTER: It's not me. My wife ain't well. My sister has got to take care of our kids, and of her. Well.

GOMM: Think of them first next time.

PORTER: It ain't as if I interfered with his medicine.

GOMM: That is exactly what it is. You may go.

PORTER: Just keeping him to look at in private. That's all. Isn't it?

SNORK *and* PORTER *exit.*

GOMM: There are priorities, Frederick. The first is discipline. Smooth is the passage to the tight ship's master. Merrick, you are safe from prying now.

TREVES: Have we nothing to say, John?

MERRICK: If all that'd stared at me'd been sacked – there'd be whole towns out of work.

TREVES: I meant, 'Thank you , sir.'

MERRICK: 'Thank you, sir.'

TREVES: We always do say please and thank you, don't we?

MERRICK: Yes, sir. Thank you.

TREVES: If we want to properly be like others.

MERRICK: Yes, sir, I want to.

TREVES: Then it is for our own good, is it not?

MERRICK: Yes, sir, Thank you, Mr Gomm.

GOMM: Sir, you are welcome. (*Exits.*)

TREVES: You are happy here, are you not, John?

19

MERRICK: Yes.

TREVES: The baths have rid you of the odour, have they not

MERRICK: First chance I had to bathe regular. Ly.

TREVES: And three meals a day delivered to your room?

ERRICK: Yes, sir.

TREVES: This is your Promised Land is it not? A roof. Food. Protection. Care. Is it not?

MERRICK: Right, Mr Treves.

TREVES: I will bet you don't know what to call this.

MERRICK: No, sir, I don't know.

TREVES: You call it, Home.

MERRICK: Never had a home before.

TREVES: You have one now. Say it, John: Home.

MERRICK: Home.

TREVES: No, no, really say it. I have a home. This is my home. Go on.

MERRICK: I have a home. This is my home. This is my home. I have a home. As long as I like?

TREVES: That is what home is.

MERRICK: That is what home is.

TREVES: If I abide by the rules, I will be happy.

MERRICK: Yes, sir.

TREVES: Don't be shy.

MERRICK: If I abide by the rules I will be happy.

TREVES: Very good. Why?

MERRICK: Why what?

TREVES: Will you be happy?

MERRICK: Because it is my home?

TREVES: No, no. Why do rules make you happy?

MERRICK: I don't know.

TREVES: Of course you do.

MERRICK: No, I really don't.

TREVES: Why does anything make you happy?

MERRICK: Like what? Like what?

TREVES: Don't be upset. Rules make us happy because they are for our own good.

MERRICK: Okay.

TREVES:Don't be shy, John. You can say it.

MERRICK: This is my home?

TREVES: No. About rules making us happy.

MERRICK: They make us happy because they are for our own good.

TREVES: Excellent. Now: I am submitting a follow-up paper on you to the London Pathological Society. It would help if you told me what you recall about your first years, John, To fill in gaps.

MERRICK: To fill in gaps. The workhouse where they put me. They beat you there like a drum. Boom boom: scrape the floor white. Shine the pan, boom boom. It never ends. The floor is always dirty. The pan is always tarnished. There is nothing you can do about it. You are always attacked anyway. Boom boom. Boom boom. Boom boom. Will the children go to the workhouse?

TREVES: What children?

MERRICK: The children. The man he sacked.

TREVES: Of necessity. Will will find other employment. You don't want crowds staring at you, do you?

MERRICK: No.

TREVES: In your own home you do not have to have crowds staring at you. Or anyone. Do you? In your home?

MERRICK: No.

TREVES: Then Mr Gomm was merciful. You yourself are proof. Is it not so? (*Pause.*) Well? Is it not so?

MERRICK: If your mercy is so cruel, what do you have for justice?

TREVES: I am sorry. It is just the way things are.

MERRICK: Boom boom. Boom boom. Boom boom.

Fadeout.

SCENE 9

MOST IMPORTANT ARE WOMEN

MERRICK *asleep, head on knees.* TREVES, MRS KENDAL *foreground.*

TREVES: You have seen photographs of John Merrick, Mrs Kendal. You are acquainted with his appearance.

MRS KENDAL: He reminds me of an audience I played Cleopatra for in Brighton once. All huge grim head and grimace and utterly unable to clap.

TREVES: Well. My aim's to lead him to as normal a life as possible. His terror of us all comes from having been held at arm's length from society. I am determined that shall end. For example, he loves to meet people and converse. I am determined he shall. For example, he had never seen the inside of any normal home before. I had him to mine, and what a reward, Mrs Kendal; his astonishment, his joy at the most ordinary things. Most critical I feel, however, are women. I will explain. They have always shown the greatest fear and loathing of him. While he adores them of course.

MRS KENDAL: Ah. He is intelligent.

TREVES: I am convinced they are the key to retrieving him from his exclusion. Though, I must warn you, women are not quite real to him – more creatures of his imagination.

MRS KENDAL. Then he is already like other men, Mr Treves.

TREVES: So I thought, an actress could help. I mean, unlike most women, you won't give in, you are trained to hide your feelings and assume others.

MRS KENDAL: You mean unlike most women I am famous for it, that is really all.

TREVES: Well. In any case. If you could enter the room and smile and wish him good morning. And when you leave, shake his hand, the left one is usable, and really quite beautiful, and say, 'I am very pleased to have made your acquaintance, Mr Merrick.'

MRS KENDAL: Shall we try it? Left hand out please. (*Suddenly radiant.*) I am *very* pleased to have made your made your acquaintance Mr Merrick. I am very *pleased* to have made your acquaintance Mr Merrick. I am very pleased to have made your *acquaintance* Mr Merrick. I *am* very pleased to have made *your* acquaintance Mr Merrick. Yes. That one.

TREVES: By god, they are all splendid. Merrick will be so pleased. It will be the day he becomes a man like other men.

MRS KENDAL: Speaking of that, Mr Treves.

TREVES: Frederick, please.

MRS KENDAL: Freddie, may I commit an indiscretion?

TREVES: Yes?

MRS KENDAL: I could not but help noticing from the

photographs that – well – of the unafflicted parts – ah, how shall I put it? (*Points to photograph.*)

TREVES: Oh. I see! I quite. Understand. No, no, no, it is quite normal.

MRS KENDAL: I thought as much.

TREVES: Medically speaking, uhm, you see the papillomatous extrusions which disfigure him, uhm, seem to correspond quite regularly to the osseous deformities, that is, excuse me, there is a link between the bone disorder and the skin growths, though for the life of me I have not discovered what it is or why it is, but in any case this – part – it would be therefore unlikely to be afflicted because well, that is, well, there's no bone in it. None in it. None at all. I mean.

MRS KENDAL: Well. Learn a little every day don't we?

TREVES: I am horribly embarrassed.

MRS KENDAL: Are you? Then he must be lonely indeed.

Fadeout.

SCENE 10

WHEN THE ILLUSION ENDS HE MUST KILL HIMSELF

MERRICK *sketching. Enter* TREVES, MRS KENDAL.

TREVES: He is making sketches for a model of St Phillip's church. He wants someday to make a model, you see.

John, my boy, this is Mrs Kendal. She would very much like to make your acquaintance.

MRS KENDAL: Good morning Mr Merrick.

TREVES: I will see to a few matters. I will be back soon. (*Exits*).

MERRICK: I planned so many things to say. I forget them. You are so beautiful.

MRS KENDAL: Good morning Mr Merrick.

MERRICK: Well. Really that was what I planned to say. That I forgot what I planned to say. I couldn't think of anything else I was so excited.

MRS KENDAL: Real charm is always planned, don't you think?

MERRICK: Well. I do not know why I look like this, Mrs Kendal. My mother was so beautiful. She was knocked down by an elephant in a circus while she was pregnant. Something must have happened, don't you think?

MRS KENDAL: It may well have.

MERRICK: It may well have. But sometimes I think my head is so big because it is so full of dreams. Because it is. Do you know what happens when dreams cannot get out?

MRS KENDAL: Why no.

MERRICK: I don't either. Something must. (*Silence*). Well, You are a famous actress.

MRS KENDAL: I am not unknown

MERRICK: You must display yourself for your living then. Like I did.

MRS KENDAL: That is not myself, Mr Merrick. That is an illusion. This is myself.

MERRICK: This is myself too.

MRS KENDAL: Frederick says you like to read. So: books

MERRICK: I am reading *Romeo and Juliet* now.

25

MRS KENDAL: Ah. Juliet. What a love story. I adore love
   stories.

MERRICK: I like love stories best too. If I had been Romeo,
   guess what.

MRS KENDAL: What?

MERRICK: I would not have held the mirror to her breath.

MRS KENDAL: You mean the scene where Juliet appears to
   be dead and he holds a mirror to her breath and sees –

MERRICK: Nothing. How does it feel when he kills himself
   because he just sees nothing?

MRS KENDAL: Well. My experience as Juliet has been –
   particularly with an actor I will not name – that while
   I'm laying there dead dead dead, and he is lamenting
   excessively, I get to thinking that if this slab of ham does
   not part from the hamhock of his life toute suite, I am
   going to scream, pop off the tomb, and plunge a dagger
   into his scene-stealing heart. Romeos are very
   undependable.

MERRICK: Because he does not care for Juliet.

MRS KENDAL: Not care?

MERRICK: Does he take her pulse? Does he get a doctor?
   Does he make sure? He kills himself. The illusion fools
   him because he does not care for her. He only cares for
   himself. If I had been Romeo, we would have got away.

MRS KENDAL: But then there would be no play, Mr Merrick.

MERRICK: If he did not love her, why should there be a
   play? Looking in a mirror and seeing nothing. That is
   not love. It was an illusion. When the illusion ended he
   had to kill himself.

MRS KENDAL: Why. That is extraordinary.

MERRICK: Before I spoke with people, I did not think of all
   these things because there was no one to bother to think

them for. Now things just come out of my mouth which are true.

TREVES *enters.*

TREVES: You are famous, John. We are in the papers. Look. They have written up my report to the Pathological Society. Look – it is a kind of apotheosis for you.

MRS KENDAL: Frederick, I feel Mr Merrick would benefit by even more company than you provide; in fact by being acquainted with the best, and they with him. I shall make it my task if you'll permit. As you know, I am a friend of nearly everyone, and I do pretty well as I please and what pleases me is this task, I think.

TREVES: By god, Mrs Kendal, you are splendid.

MRS KENDAL: Mr Merrick I must go now. I should like to return if I may. And so that we may without delay teach you about society, I would like to bring my good friend Dorothy Lady Neville. She would be most pleased if she could meet you. Let me tell her yes? (MERRICK *nods yes.*) Then until next time. I'm sure your church model will surprise us all. Mr Merrick, it has been a very great pleasure to make your acquaintance.

TREVES: John. Your hand. She wishes to shake your hand.

MERRICK: Thank you for coming.

MRS KENDAL: But it was my pleasure. Thank you. (*Exits, accompanied by* TREVES.)

TREVES: What a wonderful success. Do you know he's never shaken a woman's hand before?

> *As lights fade* MERRICK *sobs soundlessly, uncontrollably.*

Scene 11

HE DOES IT WITH JUST ONE HAND

Music. MERRICK *working on model of St Phillip's church.
Enter* DUCHESS. *At side* TREVES *ticks off a gift list.*

MERRICK: Your grace.

DUCHESS: How nicely the model is coming along, Mr Merrick. I've come to say Happy Christmas, and that I hope you will enjoy this ring and remember your friend by it.

MERRICK: Your grace, thank you.

DUCHESS: I am very pleased to have made your acquaintance. (*Exits.*)

Enter COUNTESS.

COUNTESS: Please accept these silver-backed brushes and comb for Christmas, Mr Merrick.

MERRICK: With many thanks, Countess.

COUNTESS: I am very pleased to have made your acquaintance. (*Exits.*)

Enter LORD JOHN.

LORD JOHN: Here's the silver-topped walking stick, Merrick. Make you a regular Piccadilly exquisite. Keep up the good work. Self-help is the best help. Example to us all.

MERRICK: Thank you, Lord John.

LORD JOHN: Very pleased to have made your acquaintance. (*Exits*).

Enter TREVES *and* PRINCESS ALEXANDRA.

TREVES: Her Royal Highness Princess Alexandra.

PRINCESS: The happiest of Christmases, Mr Merrick.

TREVES: Her Royal Highness has brought you a signed photograph of herself.

MERRICK: I am honoured, your Royal Highness. It is the treasure of my possessions. I have written to His Royal Highness the Prince of Wales to thank him for the pheasants and the woodcock he sent.

PRINCESS: You are a credit to Mr Treves, Mr Merrick. Mr Treves, you are a credit to medicine, to England, and to Christendom. I am so very pleased to have made your acquaintance.

PRINCESS, TREVES *exit. Enter* MRS KENDAL.

MRS KENDAL: Good news, John, Bertie says we may use the Royal Box whenever I like. Mrs Keppel says it gives a unique perspective. And for Christmas, ivory-handled razors and toothbrush.

Enter TREVES.

TREVES: And a cigarette case, my boy, full of cigarettes!

MERRICK: Thank you. Very much.

MRS KENDAL: Look Freddie, look. The model of St Phillip's.

TREVES: It is remarkable, I know.

MERRICK: And I do it with just one hand, they all say.

MRS KENDAL: You are an artist, John Merrick, an artist.

MERRICK: I did not begin to build at first. Not till I saw what St Phillip's really was. It is not stone and steel and glass; it is an imitation of grace flying up and up from the mud. So I make my imitation of an imitation. But even in that is heaven to me, Mrs Kendal.

TREVES: That thought's got a good line, John. Plato believed this was all a world of illusion and that artists made illusions of illusions of heaven.

MERRICK: You mean we are all just copies? Of originals?

TREVES: That's it.

MERRICK: Who made the copies?

TREVES: God. The Demi-urge.

MERRICK: (*Goes back to work.*) He should have used both hands shouldn't he?

Music. Puts another piece on St Phillip's. Fadeout.

SCENE 12

WHO DOES HE REMIND YOU OF?

TREVES, MRS KENDAL.

TREVES: Why all those toilet articles, tell me? He is much too deformed to use any of them.

MRS KENDAL: Props of course. To make himself. As I make me.

TREVES: You? You think of yourself.

MRS KENDAL: Well. He is gentle, almost feminine. Cheerful, honest within limits, a serious artist in his way. He is almost like me.

Enter BISHOP HOW.

30

BISHOP: He is religious and devout. He knows salvation must radiate to us or all is lost, which it's certainly not.

Enter GOMM.

GOMM: He seems practical, like me. He has seen enough of daily evil to be thankful for small goods that come his way. He knows what side his bread is buttered on, and counts his blessings for it. Like me.

Enter DUCHESS.

DUCHESS: I can speak with him of anything. For I know he is discreet. Like me.

All exit except TREVES.

TREVES: How odd. I think him curious, compassionate, concerned about the world, well, rather like myself, Freddie Treves, 1889 AD.

Enter MRS KENDAL.

MRS KENDAL: Of course he is rather odd. And hurt. And helpless not to show the struggling. And so am I.

Enter GOMM.

GOMM: He knows I use him to raise money for the London, I am certain. He understands I would be derelict if I didn't. He is wary of any promise, yet he fits in well. Like me.

Enter BISHOP HOW.

BISHOP: I as a seminarist had many of the same doubts. Struggled as he does. And hope they may be overcome.

31

Enter PRINCESS ALEXANDRA.

PRINCESS: When my husband His Royal Highness Edward Prince of Wales asked Dr Treves to be his personal surgeon, he said, 'Dear Freddie, if you can put up with the Elephant bloke, you can surely put up with me.'

All exit, except TREVES. *Enter* LORD JOHN.

LORD JOHN: See him out of fashion, Freddie. As he sees me. Social contacts critical. Oh – by the way – ignore the bloody papers; all lies. (*Exits.*)

TREVES: Merrick visibly worse than 86–87. That, as he rises higher in the consolations of society, he gets visibly more grotesque is proof definitive he is like me. Like his condition, which I make no sense of, I make no sense of mine.

Spot on MERRICK *placing another piece on St Phillip's. Fadeout.*

SCENE 13

ANXIETIES OF THE SWAMP

MERRICK, *in spot, strains to listen:* TREVES, LORD JOHN *outside.*

TREVES: But the papers are saying you broke the contracts. They are saying you've lost the money.

LORD JOHN: Freddie, if I were such a scoundrel, how would I dare face investors like yourself. Broken contracts! I

never considered them actual contracts – just preliminary
things, get the old deal under way. An actual contract's
something between gentlemen; and this attack on me
shows they are no gentlemen. Now I'm only here to say
the company remains a terribly attractive proposition.
Don't you think To recapitalize – if you could spare
another – ah. (*Enter* GOMM.) Mr Gomm. How good to
see you. Just remarking how splendidly Merrick thrives
here, thanks to you and Freddie.

GOMM: Lord John. Allow me: I must take Frederick from
you. Keep him at work. It's in his contract. Wouldn't
want him breaking it. Sort of thing makes the world fly
apart, isn't?

LORD JOHN: Yes. Well. Of course, mmm.

GOMM: Sorry to hear you're so pressed. Expect we'll see
less of you around the London now?

LORD JOHN: Of course, I, actually – ah! Overdue actually.
Appointments in the City. Freddie. Mr Gomm. (*Exits*).

TREVES: He plain fooled me. He was kind to Merrick.

GOMM: You have risen fast and easily, my boy. You've
forgotten how to protect yourself. Break now.

TREVES: It does not seem right somehow.

GOMM: The man's a moral swamp. Is that not clear yet? Is
he attractive? Deceit often is. Friendly? Swindlers can
be. Another loan? Not another cent. It may be your
money, Freddie; but I will not tolerate labouring like a
navvy that the London should represent honest charitable and compassionate science, and have titled swindlers mucking up the pitch. He has succeeded in
destroying himself so rabidly, you ought not doubt an
instant it was his real aim all along. He broke the
contracts, gambled the money away, lied, and like an

infant in his mess, gurgles and wants to do it again. Never mind details, don't want to know. Break and be glad. Don't hesitate. Today. One-man moral swamp. Don't be sucked in.

Enter MRS KENDAL.

MRS KENDAL: Have you seen the papers?

TREVES: Yes.

GOMM: Yes, yes. A great pity. Freddie: today. (*Exits.*)

MRS KENDAL: Freddie?

TREVES: He has used us. I shall be all right. Come. (MRS KENDAL, TREVES enter to MERRICK.) John: I shall not be able to stay this visit. I must, well, unravel a few things. Nurse Ireland and Snork are – ?

MERRICK: Friendly and respectful Frederick.

TREVES: I'll look in in a few days.

MERRICK: Did I do something wrong?

MRS KENDAL: No.

TREVES: This is a hospital. Not a marketplace. Don't forget it, ever. Sorry. Not you. Me. (*Exits.*)

MRS KENDAL: Well. Shall we weave today? Don't you think weaving might be fun? So many things are fun. Most men really can't enjoy them. Their loss, isn't it? I like little activities which engage me; there's something ancient in it. I don't know. Before all this. Would you like to try? John?

MERRICK: Frederick said I may stay here for life.

MRS KENDAL: And so you shall.

MERRICK: If he is in trouble?

MRS KENDAL: Frederick is your protector, John.

MERRICK: If he is in trouble? (*He picks up small photograph.*)

34

MRS KENDAL: Who is that? Ah, is it not your mother? She is pretty, isn't she?

MERRICK: Will Frederick keep his word with me, his contract, Mrs Kendal? If he is in trouble.

MRS KENDAL: What? Contract? Did you say?

MERRICK: And will you?

MRS KENDAL: I? What? Will I?

MERRICK *silent. Puts another piece on model. Fadeout.*

SCENE 14

ART IS PERMITTED BUT NATURE FORBIDDEN

Rain. MERRICK *working.* MRS KENDAL.

MERRICK: The Prince has a mistress. (*Silence.*) The Irishman had one. Everyone seems to. Or a wife. Some have both. I have concluded I need a mistress. It is bad enough not to sleep like others.

MRS KENDAL: Sitting up, you mean. Couldn't be very restful.

MERRICK: I have to. Too heavy to lay down. My head. But to sleep alone; that is worst of all.

MRS KENDAL: The artist expresses his love through his works. That is civilization.

MERRICK: Are you very shocked?

MRS KENDAL: Why should I be?

MERRICK: Others would be.

MRS KENDAL: I am not others.

MERRICK: I suppose it is hopeless.

MRS KENDAL: Nothing is hopeless. However it is unlikely.

MERRICK: I thought you might have a few ideas.

MRS KENDAL: I can guess who has ideas here.

MERRICK: You don't know something. I have never even seen a naked woman.

MRS KENDAL: Surely in all the fairs you worked.

MERRICK: I mean a real woman.

MRS KENDAL: Is one more real than another?

MERRICK: I mean like the ones in the theatre. The opera.

MRS KENDAL: Surely you can't mean they are more real.

MERRICK: In the audience. A woman not worn out early. Not deformed by awful life. A lady. Someone kept up. Respectful of herself. You don't know what fairgrounds are like, Mrs Kendal.

MRS KENDAL: You mean someone like Princess Alexandra?

MERRICK: Not so old.

MRS KENDAL: Ah. Like Dorothy.

MERRICK: She does not look happy. No.

MRS KENDAL: Lady Ellen?

MERRICK: Too thin.

MRS KENDAL: Then who?

MERRICK: Certain women. They have a kind of ripeness. They seem to stop at a perfect point.

MRS KENDAL: My dear she doesn't exist.

MERRICK: That is probably why I never saw her.

MRS KENDAL: What would your friend Bishop How say of all this I wonder?

MERRICK: He says I should put these things out of my mind.

MRS KENDAL: Is that the best he can suggest?

MERRICK: I put them out of my mind. They reappeared, snap.

MRS KENDAL: What about Frederick?

MERRICK: He would be appalled if I told him.

MRS KENDAL: I am flattered. Too little trust has maimed my life. But that is another story.

MERRICK: What a rain. Are we going to read this afternoon?

MRS KENDAL: Yes. Some women are lucky to look well, that is all. It is a rather arbitrary gift; it has no really good use, though it has uses, I will say that. Anyway it does not signify very much.

MERRICK: To me it does.

MRS KENDAL: Well. You are mistaken.

MERRICK: What are we going to read?

MRS KENDAL: Trust is very important you know. I trust you.

MERRICK: Thank you very much. I have a book of Thomas Hardy's here. He is a friend of Frederick's. Shall we read that?

MRS KENDAL: Turn around a moment. Don't look.

MERRICK: Is this a game?

MRS KENDAL: I would not call it a game. A surprise. (*She begins undressing.*)

MERRICK: What kind of a surprise?

MRS KENDAL: I saw photographs of you. Before I met you. You didn't know that, did you?

MERRICK: The ones from the first time, in '84? No, I didn't.

MRS KENDAL: I felt it was – unjust. I don't know why. I cannot say my sense of justice is my most highly developed characteristic. You may turn around again. Well. A little funny, isn't it?

MERRICK: It is the most beautiful sight I have seen. Ever.

MRS KENDAL: If you tell anyone, I shall not see you again, we shall not read, we shall not talk, we shall do nothing.

Wait. (*Undoes her hair.*) There. No illusions. Now. Well? What is there to say? 'I am extremely pleased to have made your acquaintance?'

Enter TREVES.

TREVES: For God's sakes. What is going on here? What is going on?

MRS KENDAL: For a moment, Paradise, Freddie. (*She begins dressing.*)

TREVES: But – have you no sense of decency? Woman, dress yourself quickly. (*Silence.* MERRICK *goes to put another piece on St Phillip's.*) Are you not ashamed? Do you know what you are? Don't you know what is forbidden?

Fadeout.

SCENE 15

INGRATITUDE

ROSS *in* MERRICK'S *room.*

ROSS: I come actually to ask your forgiveness.

MERRICK: I found a good home, Ross. I forgave you.

ROSS: I was hoping we could work out a deal. Something new maybe.

MERRICK: No.

ROSS: See, I was counting on it. That you were kind-hearted. Like myself. Some things don't change. Got to

put your money on the things that don't, I figure. I figure
from what I read about you, you don't change. Dukes,
Ladies coming to see you. Ask myself why? Figure it's
same as always was. Makes 'em feel good about themselves by comparison. Them things don't change. There
but for the grace of. So I figure you're selling the same
service as always. To better clientele. Difference now is
you ain't charging for it.

MERRICK: You make me sound like a whore.

ROSS: You are. I am. They are. Most are. No disgrace,
John. Disgrace is to be a stupid whore. Give it for free.
Not capitalize on the interest in you. Not to have a
manager then is stupid.

MERRICK: You see this church. I am building it. The people
who visit are friends. Not clients. I am not a dog walking
on its hind legs.

ROSS: I was thinking. Charge these people. Pleasure of the
Elephant Man's company. Something. Right spirit is
everything. Do it in the right spirit, they'd pay happily.
I'd take ten percent. I'd be okay with ten percent.

MERRICK: Bad luck's made you daft.

ROSS: I helped you, John. Discovered you. Was that daft?
No. Only daftness was being at a goldmine without a
shovel. Without proper connections. Like Treves has.
What's daft? Ross sows, Treves harvests? It's not fair, is
it John? When you think about it. I do think about it.
Because I'm old. Got something in my throat. You may
have noticed. Something in my lung here too. Something
in my belly I guess too. I'm not a heap of health, am I?
But I'd do well with ten percent. I don't need more than
ten percent. Ten percent'd give me a future slightly

39

better'n a cobblestone. This lot would pay, if you charged in the right spirit. I don't ask much.

MERRICK: They're the cream, Ross. They know it. Man like you tries to make them pay, they'll walk away.

ROSS: I'm talking about doing it in the right spirit.

MERRICK: They are my friends. I'd lose everything. For you. Ross, you lived your life. You robbed me of forty-eight pounds nine shillings, tuppence. You left me to die. Be satisfied Ross. You've had enough. You kept me like an animal in darkness. You come back and want to rob me again. Will you not be satisfied? Now I am a man like others, you want me to return?

ROSS: Had a woman yet?

MERRICK: Is that what makes a man?

ROSS: In my time it'd do for a start.

MERRICK: Not what makes this one. Yet I am like others.

ROSS: Then I'm condemned. I got no energy to try nothing new. I may well go to the dosshouse straight. Die there anyway. Between filthy dosshouse rags. Nothing in the belly but acid. I don't like pain, John. The future gives pain sense. Without a future – (*Pauses.*) Five percent? John?

MERRICK: I'm sorry, Ross. It's just the way things are.

ROSS: By god. Then I am lost.

Fadeout.

SCENE 16

NO RELIABLE GENERAL ANAESTHETIC
HAS APPEARED YET

TREVES, *reading, makes notes.* MERRICK *works.*

MERRICK: Frederick – do you believe in heaven? Hell? What about Christ? What about God? I believe in heaven. The Bible promises in heaven the crooked shall be made straight.

TREVES: So did the rack, my boy. So do we all.

MERRICK: You don't believe?

TREVES: I will settle for a reliable general anaesthetic at this point. Actually, though – I had a patient once. A woman. Operated on her for – a woman's thing. Used ether to anaesthetize. Tricky stuff. Didn't come out of it. Pulse stopped, no vital signs, absolutely moribund. Just a big white dead mackerel. Five minutes later, she fretted back to existence, like a host explorer with a great scoop of the undiscovered.

MERRICK: She saw heaven?

TREVES: Well. I quote her: it was neither heavenly nor hellish. Rather like perambulating in a London fog. People drifted by, but no one spoke. London, mind you. Hell's probably the provinces. She was shocked it wasn't more exotic. But allowed as how had she stayed, and got used to the familiar, so to speak, it did have hints of becoming a kind of bliss. She fled.

MERRICK: If you do not believe – why did you send Mrs Kendal away?

41

TREVES: Don't forget. It saved you once. My interference. You know well enough – it was not proper.

MERRICK: How can you tell? If you do not believe?

TREVES: There are still standards we abide by.

MERRICK: They make us happy because they are for our own good.

TREVES: Well. Not always.

MERRICK: Oh.

TREVES: Look, if you are angry, just say so.

MERRICK: Whose standards are they?

TREVES: I am not in the mood for this chipping away at the edges, John.

MERRICK: They do not always make us happy because they are not always for our own good?

TREVES: Everyone's. Well. Mine. Everyone's.

MERRICK: That woman's, that Juliet?

TREVES: Juliet?

MERRICK: Who died, then came back.

TREVES: Oh. I see. Yes. Her standards too.

MERRICK: So.

TREVES: So what?

MERRICK: Did you see her? Naked?

TREVES: When I was operating. Of course –

MERRICK: Oh.

TREVES: Oh what?

MERRICK: Is it okay to see them naked if you cut them up afterwards?

TREVES: Good Lord. I'm a surgeon. That is science.

MERRICK: She died. Mrs Kendal didn't.

TREVES: Well, she came back too.

MERRICK: And Mrs Kendal didn't. If you mean that.

TREVES: I am trying to read about anaesthetics. There is simply no comparison.

MERRICK: Oh.

TREVES: Science is a different thing. This woman came to me to be. I mean, it is not, well, love, you know.

MERRICK: Is that why you're looking for an anaesthetic?

TREVES: It would be a boon to surgery.

MERRICK: Because you don't love them.

TREVES: Love's got nothing to do with surgery.

MERRICK: Do you lose many patients?

TREVES: I – some.

MERRICK: Oh.

TREVES: Oh what? What does it matter? Don't you see? If I love, if any surgeon loves her or any patient or not, what does it matter? And what conceivable difference to you?

MERRICK: Because it is your standards we abide by.

TREVES: For God's sakes. If you are angry just say it. I won't turn you out. Say it: I am angry. Go on. I am angry. I am angry! I am angry!

MERRICK: I believe in heaven.

TREVES: And it is not okay. If they undress if you cut them up. As you put it. Make me sound like Jack the, Jack the Ripper.

MERRICK: No. You worry about anaesthetics.

TREVES: Are you having me on?

MERRICK: You are merciful. I myself am proof. Is it not so? (*Pauses.*) Well? Is it not so?

TREVES: Well I. About Mrs Kendal – perhaps I was wrong. I, these days that is, I seem to. Lose my head. Taking too much on perhaps. I do not know – what is in me these days.

43

MERRICK: Will she come back? Mrs Kendal?

TREVES: I will talk to her again.

MERRICK: But – will she?

TREVES: No. I don't think so.

MERRICK: Oh.

TREVES: There are other things involved. Very. That is. Other things.

MERRICK: Well. Other things. I want to walk now. Think. Other things. (*Begins to exit. Pauses.*) Why? Why won't she? (*Silence.* MERRICK *exits.*)

TREVES: Because I don't want her here when you die. (*He slumps in chair.*)

Fadeout.

SCENE 17

CRUELTY IS AS NOTHING TO KINDNESS

TREVES *asleep in chair dreams the following:* MERRICK *and* GOMM *dressed as* ROSS *in foreground.*

MERRICK: If he is merely papier mâché and paint, a swindler and a fake –

GOMM: No, no, a genuine Dorset dreamer in a moral swamp. Look – he has so forgot how to protect himself he's gone to sleep.

MERRICK: I must examine him. I would not keep him for long, Mr Gomm.

GOMM: It would be an inconvenience, Mr Merrick. He is a mainstay of our institution.

MERRICK: Exactly that brought him to my attention. I am Merrick. Here is my card. I am with the mutations across the road.

GOMM: Frederick, stand up. You must understand. He is very very valuable. We have invested a great deal in him. He is personal surgeon to the Prince of Wales.

MERRICK: But I only wish to examine him. I had not of course dreamed of changing him.

GOMM: But he is a gentleman and a good man.

MERRICK: Therefore exemplary for study as a cruel or deviant one would not be.

GOMM: Oh very well. Have him back for breakfast time or you feed him. Frederick, stand up. Up you bloody donkey, up!

TREVES, *still asleep, stands up. Fadeout.*

SCENE 18

WE ARE DEALING WITH
AN EPIDEMIC

TREVES *asleep.* MERRICK *at lecturn.*

MERRICK: The most striking feature about him, note, is the terrifying normal head. This allowed him to lie down normally, and therefore to dream in the exclusive personal manner, without the weight of others' dreams accumulating to break his neck. From the brow projected a normal vision of benevolent enlightenment, what we believe to be a kind of self-mesmerized state. The mouth, deformed by satisfaction at being at the hub of the best of existent worlds, was rendered therefore utterly incapable of self-critical speech, thus of the ability to change. The heart showed signs of worry at this unchanging yet untenable state. The back was horribly stiff from being kept against a wall to face the discontent of a world ordered for his convenience. The surgeon's hands were well-developed and strong, capable of the most delicate carvings-up, for others' own good. Due also to the normal head, the right arm was of enormous power; but, so incapable of the distinction between the assertion of authority and the charitable act of giving, that it was often to be found disgustingly beating others – for their own good. The left arm was slighter and fairer, and may be seen in typical position, hand covering the genitals which were treated as a sullen colony in constant need of restriction, governance, punishment. For their own good. To add a further burden to his trouble the wretched man when a boy developed a disabling spiritual duality, therefore was unable to feel what others feel, nor reach harmony with them. Please. (TREVES *shrugs*.) He would thus be denied all means of escape from those he had tormented.

PINS *enter*.

FIRST PIN: Mr Merrick. You have shown a profound and unknown disorder to us. You have said when he leaves here, it is for his prior life again. I do not think it ought to be permitted. It is a disgrace. It is a pity and a disgrace. It is an indecency in fact. It may be a danger in ways we do not know. Something ought to be done about it.

MERRICK: We hope in twenty years we will understand enough to put an end to this affliction.

FIRST PIN: Twenty years! Sir, that is unacceptable!

MERRICK: Had we caught it early, it might have been different. But his condition has already spread both East and West. The truth is, I am afraid, we are dealing with an epidemic.

MERRICK *puts another piece on St Phillip's.* PINS *exit.* TREVES *starts awake. Fadeout.*

SCENE 19

THEY CANNOT MAKE OUT WHAT HE IS SAYING

MERRICK, BISHOP HOW *in background.* BISHOP *gestures,* MERRICK *on knees.* TREVES *foreground. Enter* GOMM.

GOMM: Still beavering away for Christ?

TREVES: Yes.

GOMM: I got your report. He doesn't know, does he?

TREVES: The Bishop?

GOMM: I meant Merrick.

TREVES: No.

GOMM: I shall be sorry when he dies.

TREVES: It will not be unexpected anyway.

GOMM: He's brought the hospital quite a lot of good repute. Quite a lot of contributions too, for that matter. In fact, I like him; never regretted letting him stay on. Though I didn't imagine he'd last this long.

TREVES: His heart won't sustain him much longer. It may even give out when he gets off his bloody knees with that bloody man.

GOMM: What is it, Freddie? What has gone sour for you?

TREVES: It is just – it is the overarc of things, quite inescapable that he's achieved greater and greater normality, his condition's edged him closer to the grave. So – a parable of growing up? To become more normal is to die? Morc accepted to worsen? He – it is just a mockery of everything we live by.

GOMM: Sorry Freddie. Didn't catch that one.

TREVES: Nothing has gone sour. I do not know.

GOMM: Cheer up, man. You are knighted. Your clients will be kings. Nothing succeeds my boy like success. (*Exits*.)

BISHOP *comes from* MERRICK'*s room*.

BISHOP: I find my sessions with him utterly moving, Mr Treves. He struggles so. I suggested he might like to be confirmed; he leaped at it like a man lost in a desert to an oasis.

TREVES: He is very excited to do what others do if he thinks it is what others do.

BISHOP: Do you cast doubt, sir, on his faith?

TREVES: No, sir, I do not. Yet he makes all of us think he is deeply like ourselves. And yet we're not like each other. I conclude that we have polished him like a mirror, and shout hallelujah when he reflects us to the inch. I have grown sorry for it.

BISHOP: I cannot make out what you're saying. Is something troubling you, Mr Treves?

TREVES: Corsets. How about corsets? Here is a pamphlet I've written due mostly to the grotesque ailments I've seen caused by corsets. Fashion overrules me, of course. My patients do not unstrap themselves of corsets. Some cannot – you know, I have so little time in the week, I spend Sundays in the poor-wards; to keep up with work. Work being twenty-year-old women who look an abused fifty with worn-outedness; young men with appalling industrial conditions I turn out as soon as possible to return to their labours. Happily most of my patients are not poor. They are middle class. They overeat and drink so grossly, they destroy nature in themselves and all around them so fervidly, they will not last. Higher up, sir, above this middle class, I confront these same – deformities – bulged out by unlimited resources and the ruthlessness of privilege into the most scandalous dissipation yoked to the grossest ignorance and constraint. I counsel against it where I can. I am ignored of course. Then, what, sir, could be troubling me? I am an extremely successful Englishman in a successful and respected England which infroms me daily by the way it lives that it wants to die. I am in despair in fact. Science, observation, practice, deduction, having led me to these conclusions, can no longer serve as consolation. I apparently see things others don't.

BISHOP: I do wish I understood you better, sir. But as for consolation, there is in Christ's church consolation.

TREVES: I am sure we were not born for mere consolation.

BISHOP: But look at Mr Merrick's happy example.

TREVES: Oh yes. You'd like my garden too. My dog, my

wife, my daughter, pruned, cropped, pollarded and somewhat stupefied. Very happy examples, all of them. Well. Is it all we know how to finally do with – whatever? Nature? Is it? Rob it? No, not really, not nature I mean. Ourselves really. Myself really. Robbed, that is. You do see of course, can't figure out, really, what else to do with them. Can we? (*Laughs.*)

BISHOP: It is not exactly clear, sir.

TREVES: I am an awfully good gardener. Is that clear? By god I take such good care of anything, anything you, we, are convinced – are you not convinced, him I mean, is not very dangerously human? I mean how could he be? After what we've given him? What you like, sir, is that he is so grateful for patrons, so greedy to be patronized, and no demands, no rights, no hopes; past perverted, present false, future nil. What better could you ask? He puts up with all of it. Of course I do mean taken when I say given, as in what, what, what we have given him, but. You knew that. I'll bet. Because. I. I. I. I –

BISHOP: Do you mean Charity? I cannot tell what you are saying.

TREVES: Help me. (*Weeps.*)

   BISHOP *consoles him.*)

MERRICK: (*Rises, puts last piece on St Phillip's.*) It is done.

Fadeout.

SCENE 20

THE WEIGHT OF DREAMS

MERRICK *alone, looking at model. Enter* SNORK *with lunch.*

SNORK: Lunch, Mr Merrick. I'll set it up. Maybe you'd like a walk after lunch. April's doing wonders for the gardens. (*A funeral procession passes slowly by.*) My mate Will, his sister died yesterday. Twenty-eight she was. Imagine that. Wife was sick, his sister nursed her. Was a real bloom that girl. Now wife okay, sister just ups and dies. It's all so – what's that word? Forget it. It means chance-y. Well. Forgot it. Chance-y'll do. Have a good lunch. (*Exits.*)

MERRICK *eats a little, breathes on model, polishes it, goes to bed, arms on knees, head on arms, the position in which he must sleep.*)

MERRICK: Chancey? (*Sleeps.*)

Enter PINHEADS *singing.*)

PINS:

We are the Queens of the Cosmos
Beautiful darkness' empire
Darkness darkness, light's true flower,
Here is eternity's finest hour
sleep like others you learn to admire
Be like your mother, be like your sire.

They straighten MERRICK *out to normal sleep position.*

His head tilts over too far. His arms fly up clawing the air. He dies. As light fades, SNORK *enters.*

SNORK: I remember it, Mr Merrick. The world is 'arbitrary.' Arbitrary. It's all so – oh. Hey! Hey! The Elephant Man is dead!

Fadeout.

SCENE 21

FINAL REPORT TO THE INVESTORS

GOMM *reading,* TREVES *listening.*

GOMM: 'To the Editor of the *Times*. Sir; In November, 1886, you were kind enough to insert in the *Times* a letter from me drawing attention to the case of Joseph Merrick – '

TREVES: John. John Merrick.

GOMM: Well. ' – known as the Elephant Man. It was one of singular and exceptional misfortune' et cetera et cetera '. . . debarred from earning his livelihood in any other way than being exhibited to the gaze of the curious. This having been rightly interfered with by the police . . .' et cetera et cetera, 'with great difficulty he succeeded somehow or other in getting to the door of the London Hospital where through the kindness of one of our surgeons he was sheltered for a time.' And then . . . and then . . . and . . . ah. 'While deterred by common humanity from evicting him again into the open street, I wrote to you and from that moment all difficulty vanished; the sympathy of many was aroused, and although no other fitting refuge was offered, a sufficient sum was placed at my disposal, apart from the funds of the hospital, to maintain him for what did not promise to be a prolonged life. As – '

TREVES: I forgot. The coroner said it was death by asphyxiation. The weight of the head crushed the windpipe.

GOMM: Well. I go on to say about how he spent his time here, that all attempted to alleviate his misery, that he was visited by the highest in the land et cetera, et cetera, that in general he joined our lives as best he could, and 'In spite of all this indulgence, he was quiet and unassuming, grateful for all that was done for him, and conformed readily to the restrictions which were necessary.' Will that do so far, do you think?

TREVES: Should think it would.

GOMM: Wouldn't add anything else, would you?

TREVES: Well. He was highly intelligent. He had an acute sensibility; and worst for him, a romantic imagination. No, no. Never mind. I am really not certain of any of it. (*Exits*).

GOMM: 'I have given these details thinking that those who sent money to use for his support would like to know how their charity was used. Last Friday afternoon, though apparently in his usual health, he quietly passed away in his sleep. I have left in my hands a small balance of the money for his support, and this I now propose after paying certain gratuities, to hand over to the general funds of the hospital. This course I believe will be consonant with the wishes of the contributors.

'It was the courtesy of the *Times* in inserting my letter in
1886 that procured me this afflicted man a comfortable
protection during the last years of a previously wretched
existence, and I desire to take this opportunity of thank-
fully acknowledging it.

'I am, sir, your obedient servant,

F. C. Carr Gomm

'House Committee Room, London Hospital.'

15 April 1890.

TREVES *re-enters*.

TREVES: I did think of one small thing.

GOMM: It's too late, I'm afraid. It is done. (*Smiles*.)

Hold before fadeout.

ACTIVITIES AND EXPLORATIONS

A Keeping Track

Scene 1

1 Why has Frederick Treves come to the London Hospital?
2 Describe Treves's background.
3 What does Mr Carr tell Treves about the London Hospital and about what Treves can expect in the future?

Scene 2

1 What does Ross *say* his reasons are for displaying John Merrick to the public?
2 What do you think his *real* attitude to Merrick is? Can you find evidence to support your view?
3 How much do you learn about Merrick's background?
4 What is Treves's interest in Merrick? What does he arrange to do?

Scene 3

1 Treves compares many of Merrick's deformities to vegetable qualities. Identify these images. What do you learn of Treves's attitudes from the language he uses?
2 What views are expressed in this scene by the 'Voice'? Who does this voice represent, do you think?

Scene 4

1 Why have Ross and Merrick come to Belgium?
2 Who are the 'Pinheads'? Why are they more acceptable to the public than Merrick?
3 Merrick repeatedly uses the word 'robbed' towards the end of this scene. Can you see more than one meaning here?

Scene 5

1 Why is Merrick threatened by the mob?
2 Comment on the Policeman's remark, 'People who think right don't look like that, do they?'
3 When Merrick says 'Jesus' the Policeman thinks he is saying 'Treves'. Do you think the author is making a particular point here?

Scene 6

1 Treves makes a point of telling Miss Sandwich that Merrick has a 'disorder' not a 'disease'. Explain the difference between the two words.
2 Why exactly has John Merrick's appearance 'terrified' other nurses? What do they believe caused John's disorder?
3 How does Miss Sandwich react when she sees John?
4 How does John respond to her horror?

Scene 7

1 What does Bishop How see in John?
2 What news does Gomm bring? How have the public changed their attitude towards John Merrick?
3 What does the Bishop say about Treves's motives for helping John? Do you think the Bishop is right?
4 What do you think Gomm is hinting at in the last lines of the scene?

Scene 8

1 Why does John want to live in a home for the blind?
2 What does Treves mean when he says that the Porter has 'interfered' with John's medicine?
3 Treves says that he has brought John to the 'Promised Land' by providing him with 'A roof. Food. Protection.'

These things, he says, make a 'home'. Do you think the author intends an irony here?

4 What point is Merrick making in his story about the workhouse?

Scene 9

1 Why has Treves brought Mrs Kendal to meet John? Do you think his explanation to her, about why John needs to meet a woman, is a correct interpretation of John's feelings?

2 When Treves says that he is 'horribly embarrassed', Mrs Kendall comments that John must be 'lonely indeed'. What does she mean?

Scene 10

1 What do John and Mrs Kendall have in common?

2 Can you see how John's comments about 'Romeo and Juliet' might apply to himself?

3 Look up the word, 'apotheosis'. Do you believe that Treves's report to the Pathological Society really is an apotheosis for John?

4 Why do you think John 'sobs' at the end of the scene?

Scene 11

1 Look closely at what John's visitors say. Why are they visiting him?

2 Can you explain why John is making a model of St Phillip's?

Scene 12

1 In this scene you learn more about John's visitors. What do they see in John? Illustrate your answer with quotations from the text.

2 Look at Treves's last speech in this scene. What does Treves perceive is happening to him?

Scene 13

1 How has Lord John 'used' Treves?
2 Is the author suggesting in this scene that Treves is in some way 'breaking the contract' between Treves and John Merrick?
3 What do you think is being said about Victorian society in this scene?
4 Why do you think Merrick looks at his mother's photograph as he worries about Treves?

Scene 14

1 Do you think that Mrs Kendall is right to act as she does in this scene?
2 Does her action make her response to John in any way different from how all the other characters see him?
3 How does her action illustrate her 'sense of justice'?
4 Comment on Treves's reaction to what he sees.
5 What do you think is being said here about 'art and nature'?

Scene 15

1 Ross says 'Some things don't change'. Explain what he is saying about the connections between himself and Treves.
2 How does John argue that things *have* changed for him?

Scene 16

1 Treves describes heaven as 'a London fog', and God as 'a reliable general anaesthetic'. What does this suggest about his beliefs – or the way he sees life?

2 If Treves does not really believe in heaven, what does he believe in?

3 What point do you think John is making when he implies that Treves wants to find an anaesthetic for himself, rather than his patients?

4 At the end of the scene, after John has left, Treves says that he does not want Mrs Kendall to be present when John dies. Is this compassion, or is there more to it than that?

Scene 17 and Scene 18

1 In Treves's dream he changes places with John. Can you explain how he dreams that he is the 'freak'?

Scene 19

1 What does Treves say is killing John?

2 Treves says 'we have polished him like a mirror.' How does this comment relate to earlier scenes in the play?

3 How does Treves's talk of corsets fit in here? What is Treves saying about his society?

4 Treves describes himself as 'an awfully good gardener'. What does he mean?

5 The word 'robbed' is used again, (see Scene 4). What has John been robbed of?

6 Treves's last line, 'Help me', is also an echo from earlier in the play. Can you identify the connection?

Scene 20

1 How is Merrick's death the final illustration of everything Treves has said in the previous scene?

2 Has his death been 'arbitrary' or is this intended as an irony by the author?

Scene 21

1 What does Gomm's letter tell you about the hospital's final reaction to John's stay with them?
2 What do you think the 'one small thing' is that Treves remembers?

B Explorations

1 Interviews

(a) Ask John Merrick's mother about John's birth and early life. Try to get her to explain why she left him in the workhouse when he was three.
(b) Interview John Merrick about his early life. Include the years he spent with Ross.
(c) Question Frederick Treves about his 'treatment' of John Merrick. Try to discover his aims, the key events of this time with John and whether he thinks his approach has been successful.

2 Diaries

(a) John Merrick's diary. Write three entries, (i) on his arrival at the London Hospital: the events leading up to this moment, his impressions of Treves and Gomm, his hopes for the future; (ii) his impressions of London society – why they visit him, how he feels about them and his feelings towards Mrs Kendall, and how she differs from the others; (iii) just before his death – how he feels about Treves and his experiences at the Hospital – is there anything *more* he would have liked out of life? (You might date these entries in 1886, 1889 and 1890.)
(b) Frederick Treves's diary. Three entries, (i) on his early meetings with John, what he hopes to do for him and how this might help his own future; (ii) on what he is

trying to teach John, and how much impact John is having on London society; (iii) on the doubts he is having about how successful he has been with John – and with his whole career; he might recount his bad dreams in this entry. (The dates for these entries could be as for John's diary, except the last might be shortly before John's death.)

3 Letters

(a) Write a letter from John's mother in which she explains to John why she left him and how she feels about what she has done. Alongside this, write John's reply.

(b) Write a letter from John to the local newspaper in which he describes how he felt when he was in the fair as a 'sideshow'. What does he think of the way people have reacted to him throughout his life?

(c) Write a letter from Frederick Treves to a medical journal. The subject of his letter might be a summary of the 'causes' of (i.e. superstitions about) John's disorder and how he believes John should be treated.

4 Poems

Have a look at a poem called 'The Hunchback in the Park' (in *The Poems*, by Dylan Thomas). Can you see a connection between the character described in the poem and John Merrick? Using what you know about John's experiences, feelings and dreams, write, 'John Merrick's Poem'.

Similarly, you might read a poem called 'In the Snack Bar' by Edwin Morgan (in a Penguin books entitled *Worlds, Seven Modern Poets*). Using Frederick Treves's concerns about and attitudes to John as your starting point, write 'Frederick Treves's Poem'.

5 Story – the betrayal

Imagine a situation where Frederick Treves and Ross meet a short time after the events of the play. Perhaps Ross is seriously ill and is admitted to the London Hospital and Frederick is his doctor. They discuss how they both feel they have 'betrayed' John Merrick, during his life. Would either of them do things differently given a second chance?

6 Plays for today

Here are two ideas for short plays – which your group might like to develop for another class to see, or even for a school assembly.

(a) A group of young people are depressed and unhappy because they have just seen a number of disabled children in the local shopping centre. They feel really sorry for them. A doctor appears, examines the depressed group and diagnoses *guilt*. (Perhaps he hangs labels on them – GUILT). They beg for a remedy. The doctor reveals that he has a special mixture, it's called 'Give a few pennies to help the disabled'. He takes out a huge syringe, injects them all and they depart happy.

Before the doctor has a chance to leave he is intercepted by a young disabled person (perhaps blind, or in a wheelchair) who asks if the doctor can help his or her illness. The doctor apologises and says finding a cure would be much too expensive. The disabled person asks, if no cure can be found then can the doctor prescribe something to help him/her live a life like the others? Again the doctor protests that this would cost too much money.

The final line of the play might be 'Who are we trying to cure?'

Discussion: What is the play saying about giving donations on flag days or undertaking the occasional sponsored event to help the disabled?

(b) A person struggles on, 'disabled' by a huge ball and chain around his or her leg. A group of young people appear and decide that what this disabled person needs is a decent place to live and enough food to eat. They present an umbrella and an apple, then go on their way. The disabled person puts up the umbrella and eats the apple. Another group of young people appear – obviously students. They decide that what the disabled person needs is a good education. They hand over their books and go on their way. The disabled person looks at the books.

A group of young medical students arrive. They decide that the problem is the poor general health of the disabled person, and prescribe plenty of rest and freedom from worry. As the disabled person has no money they give him or her an aspirin and move on.

(Others might pass by – a clergyman, a businessman, etc. with similar effect).

Finally, a group of young people appear; among them is another disabled person, who gives the first disabled individual a present. It is a file (for filing through the chain). The file, she says, will liberate him.

Discussion: What does the file mean? How can we give a liberating file to the disabled?

Final question following both of these plays: Is charity enough to bring about a real change in the lives of the people we want to help?

7 Project: John Merrick and Me

Think about your community, your local area, your school, your class – and the people in your immediate environment who might feel left out in one way or another, like John Merrick in the play. The degree of isolation might vary enormously, from the socially awkward person in school, to the seriously ill in your community. Your survey of such people might include the bullied, the mentally ill, the disabled.

Are the people you identify being looked after? If so, how? If not, what do you think they need? Is it just a matter of practical help (like ramps for wheelchairs for instance)? Or is it more than this? Think again about what John Merrick needed in the play.

How might the people you have discussed in your community be given the support they need?

Your project might fall into three main sections: (i) What is the situation in my community? (ii) What is being done? (iii) What should be done now?

In other words, what have you discovered in the story of John Merrick which might apply to society's idea of what is 'normal'?

C Essays

1 What does The Elephant Man tell us about what Victorians thought caused disabilities like John Merrick's? Look closely at Scenes 5 and 6 to help you with your answer.

2 How does the general public's attitude towards John Merrick change during the course of the play? How do you explain this change?

3 In 1967 Lord Florey said:

'People sometimes think that I and the others who worked on penicillin did so because we were interested in suffering humanity – I don't think it ever crossed our minds about suffering humanity; this was an interesting scientific exercise.'

How far do these views reflect Frederick Treves's attitude to John Merrick?

4 On the surface Frederick Treves is a successful man, yet much of the time he seems deeply unhappy. Discuss this apparent contradiction.

5 How important to the theme of *The Elephant Man* is Frederick Treves's dream?

6 'Mrs Kendall is the only character with the courage to break with the pseudo-morality of her time.' Examine this statement and say how far you agree with it.

7 What does Treves do to, and for, John Merrick in the play? How does Merrick respond to the 'treatment' he receives?

8 '*The Elephant Man* is concerned with appearances and how they deceive.' Discuss.

9 'I believe the building of the church model constitutes some kind of central metaphor, and groping towards conditions where it can be built and the building of it are the action of the play.' (Bernard Pomerance). Explain and illustrate this comment.

10 Discuss the play's criticisms of Victorian society and consider how far you think Bernard Pomerance's observations apply today.